D0491314

H...
B...

©...

IS...

Item: 005602630

Dewey Decimal Classification Number: 241

Subject Heading: BELIEF AND DOUBT \ CHRISTIAN ETHICS \ HONESTY

Eric Geiger
Vice President, Church Resources

Ronnie Floyd
General Editor

David Francis
Managing Editor

Gena Rogers
Karen Dockrey
Content Editors

Philip Nation
Director, Adult Ministry Publishing

Faith Whatley
Director, Adult Ministry

Send questions/comments to: Content Editor, *Bible Studies for Life: Adults*, One LifeWay Plaza, Nashville, TN 37234-0175; or make comments on the Web at *www.BibleStudiesforLife.com*.

Printed in the United States of America

For ordering or inquiries, visit *www.lifeway.com*; write LifeWay Small Groups; One LifeWay Plaza; Nashville, TN 37234-0152; or call toll free (800) 458-2772.

All Scripture quotations, unless otherwise indicated, are taken from the Holman Christian Standard Bible®, copyright 1999, 2000, 2002, 2003, 2009 by Holman Bible Publishers. Used by permission.

Bible Studies for Life: Adults often lists websites that may be helpful to our readers. Our staff verifies each site's usefulness and appropriateness prior to publication. However, website content changes quickly so we encourage you to approach all websites with caution. Make sure sites are still appropriate before sharing them with students, friends, and family.

Social Media

Connect with a community of *Bible Studies for Life* users. Post responses to questions, share teaching ideas, and link to great blog content.
Facebook.com/BibleStudiesForLife

Get instant updates about new articles, giveaways, and more. *@BibleMeetsLife*

The App

Simple and straightforward, this elegantly designed iPhone app gives you all the content of the Small Group Member Book—plus a whole lot more—right at your fingertips. Available in the iTunes App Store; search **"Bible Studies for Life."**

Blog

At *BibleStudiesForLife.com/blog* you will find magazine articles and music downloads from LifeWay Worship. Plus, leaders and group members alike will benefit from the blog posts written for people in every life stage—singles, parents, boomers, and senior adults—as well as media clips, connections between our study topics, current events, and much more.

Can we know the truth? Or is everything relative?

Living the Christian life as "strangers and aliens" in this world has been a challenge for believers in every century. Truth is seen by some as an outdated and irrelevant concept. Sources formerly unquestioned have now been dismissed as unreliable.

In fact, one of the most popular teachings of our day is that you can't know the truth about anything because truth is a relative term. Can we know the truth? Do absolutes still exist? Christians believe that God Himself is true and is an unfailing source of truthfulness. He has given us His Word and in that Word we learn of Him who is the Way, the Truth, and the Life.

Christians in the 21st century need to know what they believe and why they believe it. The six sessions of *Honest to God* will enable you to grow in your own faith and equip you to be more effective in sharing that faith with others. These sessions address foundational issues in the life of every person:

▶ The origin and significance of human life

▶ The existence and nature of God

▶ How God reveals Himself and relates to people

Studying chapters of Scripture like Genesis 1, Job 42, Psalms 19, 119, and 139, and Romans 1 will enrich your life and adjust your perspective. You will learn what the Bible really says on crucial matters in a way that is both refreshing and honest.

Robert Jeffress

Robert Jeffress is senior pastor of the First Baptist Church of Dallas, Texas. Robert is known for a biblical and practical approach that has made him one of the country's most respected evangelical leaders. Dr. Jeffress is the author of *How Can I Know?* (LifeWay, 2012), a study that examines in-depth seven tough questions people ask.

Dr. Jeffress graduated from Baylor University (B.A.), Dallas Theological Seminary (Th.M.), and Southwestern Baptist Theological Seminary (D.Min.). He resides in Dallas with his wife, Amy. They are the parents of two daughters, Julia and Dorothy.

contents

SESSION 1

IS EVERY LIFE SACRED?

How can people tell what is valuable to you?

God values life and so should we.

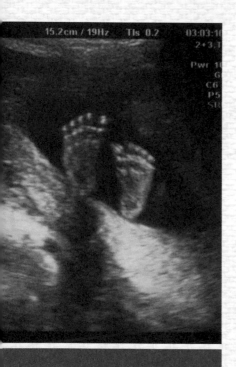

THE BIBLE MEETS LIFE

What is the value of a human life? For many in our American culture, a mother's womb has become a hazardous site. The plight of the aged is riddled with accounts of neglect and abuse.

More than 25 years ago, former Surgeon General, C. Everett Koop lamented the devaluation of human life, "When I graduated from medical school the idea was, 'How can I save this life?' but now for a great number of the medical students it is, 'Should I save this life?'" If we want to understand the true value of life, the best resource to consult is the book penned by the Author of life.

The God of creation, who created us in His image, provides us with several insights into His perspective about the incalculable worth of human life. One specific example of this perspective is found in Psalm 139. Addressed to the Choirmaster, this psalm of David celebrates God's intimate knowledge of us and His intricate fashioning of us as His unique handiwork. As the Author and Sustainer of human life, God values our existence. Because He values life, so should we.

WHAT DOES THE BIBLE SAY?

Psalm 139:1-6,13-18 *(HCSB)*

1 LORD, You have searched me and known me.

2 You know when I sit down and when I stand up; You understand my thoughts from far away.

3 You observe my travels and my rest; You are aware of all my ways.

4 Before a word is on my tongue, You know all about it, LORD.

5 You have encircled me; You have placed Your hand on me.

6 This extraordinary knowledge is beyond me. It is lofty; I am unable to reach it.

13 For it was You who created my inward parts; You knit me together in my mother's womb.

14 I will praise You because I have been remarkably and wonderfully made. Your works are wonderful, and I know this very well.

15 My bones were not hidden from You when I was made in secret, when I was formed in the depths of the earth.

16 Your eyes saw me when I was formless; all my days were written in Your book and planned before a single one of them began.

17 God, how difficult Your thoughts are for me to comprehend; how vast their sum is!

18 If I counted them, they would outnumber the grains of sand; when I wake up, I am still with You.

Key Words

known (v. 1)—Unique kind of intimate knowledge of a person resulting from a close, personal relationship; how the Lord knows us.

encircled (v. 5)—Being enfolded back and front by the Lord, who has the absolute power to control and protect completely.

knit me (v. 13)—Depicts a skilled artisan, carefully weaving a tapestry with exact precision. It pictures God's intimate involvement in creating each of us.

Psalm 139:1-6

David marveled at the Lord's comprehensive knowledge and awareness of him. The God who created us and who has a plan for us is also the God who is with us wherever we might be. God is always present with His people. God is mindful of our daily schedules, activities, and thoughts. He goes before us and behind us.

The Lord's presence is inescapable. We never go anywhere, engage in any activity, or entertain any thought outside of the knowledge and presence of God. God is neither unconcerned with humanity, nor distant.

Some people may picture God as a supreme being who takes no active interest in His creation. To them, God may seem detached and distant, unwilling to empathize with the experiences and emotions of His creatures.

Yet, the Bible presents God as One who actively intervenes in the lives of people. For example, consider Moses' first encounter with God described in Exodus 3. When the Lord called him to be the deliverer of His people, Moses was overwhelmed. God revealed His presence to Moses at the burning bush, through the Red Sea, and on the top of Mount Sinai, demonstrating that He was always with His people.

In the nativity story, we see the focus on God's presence taken to an entirely new level. The Son born to a virgin is described as Immanuel, a name meaning "God with us." Jesus was the Word made flesh who came to earth to save His people. Later, when Jesus charged His disciples to go into the entire world with the good news of the gospel, He included this promise: "I am with you always, to the end of the age" (Matt. 28:20). God will never leave us nor forsake us (see Heb. 13:5).

From these verses, how can you know that God values you?

QUESTION **#1**

EXPRESSING VALUE

Choose one

Ways I can show love to these people:

- ☐ Unborn children
- ☐ Children and students
- ☐ Elderly adults
- ☐ People with physical challenges
- ☐ People with mental challenges

Psalm 139:13-16

The fact that God has developed a detailed plan for every aspect of our existence is further proof of our worth to Him. David recognized that he had been fearfully and wonderfully made:

▶ God Himself is the Source and Designer of our existence.

▶ He formed our inward parts and knit us in the womb.

If we take these verses seriously, we are left with no other option than the reality that human life begins at conception. We do not need a medical degree to understand that a life in embryonic form is a life and not a meaningless blob. These verses reveal the stunning contrast between God's view of human life and the view that fueled the landmark decision, Roe v. Wade, which legalized abortion in 1973. According to the federal Centers for Disease Control and Prevention, more than 50 million abortions have been performed in the United States since 1973.*

"But what about those children born with disabilities or deformities?" These realities are a part of humanity's fallen state. We live in a world marred by sin in which Satan, the prince of darkness, wields his wicked influence. All of creation has been affected by sin. Yet this truth in no way justifies the extermination of those deemed by a society to be unfit or unproductive. History is replete with the stories of those who bless others and make significant contributions even in the midst of their disabilities.

The human body, with all of its members and functions, is an astoundingly complex and amazingly orchestrated creation.

The Lord created us, and orchestrated and ordered all the days of our lives. Given these truths, it is no wonder that David erupted in praise and wonder, "Your works are wonderful" (v. 14).

* Based on the CDC's Annual Abortion Surveillance Reports (*www.cdc.gov*)

Since life begins at conception, how does this impact our attitudes toward the hardest questions about abortion?

QUESTION **#2**

What should characterize our treatment of others (the sick, poor, disabled, elderly) in light of the fact that we are all fearfully and wonderfully made?

QUESTION **#3**

> "How far you go in life depends on your being tender with the young, compassionate with the aged, sympathetic with the striving and tolerant of the weak and strong. Because someday in your life you will have been all of these."

— GEORGE WASHINGTON CARVER

Psalm 139:17-18

We should live in light of the fact that God values us. He has assigned worth to those made in His image. Jesus confirmed the truth that God values human life: "Aren't five sparrows sold for two pennies? Yet not one of them is forgotten in God's sight. Indeed, the hairs of your head are all counted. Don't be afraid; you are worth more than many sparrows!" (Luke 12:6-7).

Beyond that, God also knows us completely. Our past, present, and future actions and thoughts are seen by an all-powerful and all-knowing God. This knowledge blew David's mind. He couldn't wrap his finite mind around the reality that the Lord, so lofty and transcendent, has taken such an intense and intimate interest in him.

God's love and care for us is particularly amazing, given that He knows everything about us—the good, the bad, and the ugly. God knew the worst about David and He knows the worst about us. Yet, because of His love and grace, He values us and sets His love upon us anyway.

The ultimate demonstration of God's valuing of us is the cross of Jesus Christ. "But God proves His own love for us in that while we were still sinners, Christ died for us" (Rom. 5:8).

The sacredness of human life is grounded in the facts that God created us in His image, knows every detail of our existence, and has given His Son in order to save us from our sins.

Which attribute of God mentioned in these verses have you recently seen firsthand?

QUESTION #4

LIVE IT OUT

Psalm 139 shows that God values human life. So should we.

▶ **Write a letter that values life**. Perhaps you'll enclose money to help save babies and enhance lives. Your local school might need a piece of playground equipment that accommodates a child who happens to be in a wheelchair.

▶ **Show grace**. Many people suffer silently with guilt over involvement with a past abortion. If you know someone like this, extend God's love and grace to him or her.

▶ **Form a friendship with someone who's been labeled**. Think about the labels "homeless," "terminally ill," "mentally handicapped," and so on. Getting to know someone will change your attitude about that person.

God calls us to value, cherish, and guard human life. Show the sanctity of each life.

The Lost Voices

I can't do this! I can't be in a Bible study with all these godly women. I don't fit in here, Sandy thought, wiping mascara-stained tears from her face. I've had four abortions. How can God forgive that when I can't forgive myself? These women would be appalled if they knew my secret.

Can you picture the church, God's family of faith, as the scariest place in the world to share your deepest secret and greatest pain? Perhaps you can.

To continue reading "The Lost Voices" from *HomeLife* magazine, visit *BibleStudiesforLife.com/articles*.

My group's prayer requests

....

....

....

....

....

....

....

....

....

....

My thoughts

SESSION 2

HOW CAN I BE SURE GOD EXISTS?

What architecture, music, or marvel moves you?

God has given us ways to know Him.

THE BIBLE MEETS LIFE

Does God really exist?

Polls reveal that an increasing number of people question or deny the existence of God. Today, belief in God is no longer assumed or valued. From the fields of science to sociology, we hear voices declaring that we no longer need God and that He is simply a figment of the imagination.

In this climate many are asking the question, "How can I know God exists?" It is impossible to "prove" the existence—or the non-existence—of God. But the real question is, "Does the evidence around us argue for or against the existence of a divine Creator?" Just as a spectacular building or an inspiring piece of music draws us to the one who designed or wrote it, Psalm 19 argues that creation itself testifies to the reality of God, reflecting both the existence and attributes of our Creator.

WHAT DOES THE BIBLE SAY?

Psalm 19:1-14 *(HCSB)*

1 The heavens declare the glory of God, and the sky proclaims the work of His hands.

2 Day after day they pour out speech; night after night they communicate knowledge.

3 There is no speech; there are no words; their voice is not heard.

4 Their message has gone out to all the earth, and their words to the ends of the world. In the heavens He has pitched a tent for the sun.

5 It is like a groom coming from the bridal chamber; it rejoices like an athlete running a course.

6 It rises from one end of the heavens and circles to their other end; nothing is hidden from its heat.

7 The instruction of the LORD is perfect, renewing one's life; the testimony of the LORD is trustworthy, making the inexperienced wise.

8 The precepts of the LORD are right, making the heart glad; the command of the LORD is radiant, making the eyes light up.

9 The fear of the LORD is pure, enduring forever; the ordinances of the LORD are reliable and altogether righteous.

10 They are more desirable than gold—than an abundance of pure gold; and sweeter than honey, which comes from the honeycomb.

11 In addition, Your servant is warned by them; there is great reward in keeping them.

12 Who perceives his unintentional sins? Cleanse me from my hidden faults.

13 Moreover, keep Your servant from willful sins; do not let them rule over me. Then I will be innocent and cleansed from blatant rebellion.

14 May the words of my mouth and the meditation of my heart be acceptable to You, LORD, my rock and my Redeemer.

Key Words

glory (v. 1)—The full spectrum of God's marvelous attributes displayed in His creation and actions.

precepts (v. 8)—The expectations that God has given His people so they can live in freedom and joy.

fear (v. 9)—The response to God's instruction that includes obedience to Him with an attitude of reverence, love, and humility.

Psalm 19:1-6

David showed how creation testifies to the existence of God. His strong verbs highlight this fact:

▶ Declare

▶ Proclaims

▶ Pour out

▶ Communicate

The atmospheric heavens are said to declare God's glory. The Hebrew term for "glory" refers to God's weightiness. God is not a "lightweight." He is a God of greatness and grandeur. In the second part of verse 1, David reinforces the first part of the verse with a parallel statement. The sky above proclaims the handiwork of God. Looking into the sky above reminded David of the One behind it.

In verse 2, David shifts attention to the orderly pattern and transition from day to night. He employed poetic language to describe the sun's rising: it comes out of its "tent" like a bridegroom leaving his chamber. Verse 6 pictures the path of the sun as it moves from one end of the heavens to the other, likening it to an "athlete" who runs his course with joy, so that nothing is hidden from its warmth or heat.

We may take for granted the splendor and beauty of what God has created. Getting up to catch the rising of the sun can be a true worship experience as we are reminded of God's vast arsenal of power and our own limited resources and perspectives. Observing the night sky on a clear night and the stars that twinkle on its canvas can awaken us to the transcendence and magnitude of the God of creation.

> *Creation can tell us about God's eminence (His dominion over creation), but what can it tell us about His imminence (His nearness)?*
>
> QUESTION #1

> *If nature reveals God so clearly, why do we sometimes struggle to believe?*
>
> QUESTION #2

Psalm 19:7-11

The sky and sun are but two examples of God revealing Himself through nature. These natural and physical realities are not to be worshiped; rather, we worship the God who created them. As astounding and remarkable as God's creation is, it only goes so far in providing what we need to know about God.

▶ **General Revelation**. Up to this point, we've been looking at how God has revealed Himself in a general sense through nature.

▶ **Special Revelation**. God has also revealed Himself by direct communication to people. This special revelation is deposited in God's Word—the Bible. David offered a series of parallel statements which describe the wonder and value of God's Word: instruction, testimony, command, fear, precepts, and ordinances.

These synonyms vividly illustrate the impact of God's spoken revelation. The Lord's words are "perfect" or "blameless"; as such, they bring restoration to people down to the core of their beings. The Lord's "precepts" or statutes are "right" and morally consistent. They lead a heart to rejoice. Likewise, because the commandment of the Lord is pure, it enlightens the eyes. Because God's Word is so crucial to cultivating a proper view and reverence for Him, David called it the "fear of the Lord." The Word of God is also a protective shield, preventing sin. To know God better, know the Scripture that reveals Him.

> *What does the Bible reveal about God that nature does not?*

QUESTION #3

Psalm 19:12-14

▶ God's Word accurately reveals the one true God.

▶ God's Word gives us objective insight into His character and attributes.

A survey by the American Bible Society revealed that 88 percent of American homes have at least one Bible.* In America, we have unlimited opportunity to read God's Word. Instead of taking this privilege for granted, we should saturate ourselves with the Bible.

We must respond to God's revelation with our hearts and minds. David certainly knew through his own successes and failures the importance of heeding the revelation of God. David acknowledged the inability of humans to discern truth and error apart from God's Word. Aware of his own hidden or unknown faults, David desired to be declared innocent.

> *How does the existence of God impact the way you approach each day?*
>
> QUESTION #4

In verse 13, David made a request that should be a regular item on our prayer list: to be kept back from "willful sins." This refers to our abuse of God's grace by continuing to do what we know is wrong. David pleaded with God to keep him from presuming upon God's grace. He desired to be super-sensitive rather than callous toward sin.

David was rightly horrified at the prospect of sin ruling over his life. A disregard for disobedience to God leads to a loss of direction in life. Lacking proper discernment, we move down paths God has clearly marked "off limits" for our own protection.

David concluded with another personal request. He asked that the words which proceed from his mouth might be acceptable (pleasing) in God's sight. He wanted to honor the God who graciously and clearly has spoken in Scripture. David also prayed that the meditations or thoughts of his heart be acceptable in God's sight. "Heart" in this verse refers to that center of one's personality from which thoughts and feelings flow. Internally and externally, David sought to honor God.

* American Bible Society: "State of the Bible 2013" (*www.AmericanBible.org*)

*"You can see God from anywhere
if your mind is set
to love and obey Him."*

—A.W. TOZER

NURTURING FAITH

1. The aspect of God that most impresses me is . . .

_____

_____

_____

2. The feature of God's Word that most impresses me is . . .

_____

_____

_____

3. A way God and His Word nurture my walk is . . .

_____

_____

_____

LIVE IT OUT

God has provided us with powerful clues, in nature and His Word, about His existence and greatness. How will you respond to His revelation?

▶ **Look around**. Look up at the sky or at nature around you. What do you see that indicates God is real?

▶ **Join the chorus**. Seek to live your life so that it joins creation in declaring the glory of God. Let your actions point to God.

▶ **Express your faith**. Explain to someone why you believe God is real based on both nature and Scripture. When you put your convictions into words, you grasp better the truth you hold inwardly.

God desires more than a simple acknowledgement of His reality. He wants us to have a true relationship with Him and to build our lives around Him. Look above. Look in Scripture.

Shadow of a Doubt

I had the privilege of growing up in church. When I was 8, I distinctly remember realizing that God was drawing me to Himself. I embraced Jesus as my Savior and entered into new life in the family of God. Though that day was almost 25 years ago, I can still remember the emotions I felt, who was there with me, even exactly what I prayed. I remember how excited I was. But those days on the mountain of excitement and joy didn't last long. They quickly faded into a dark valley of doubt.

To continue reading "Shadow of a Doubt" from *HomeLife* magazine, visit *BibleStudiesforLife.com/articles*.

My group's prayer requests

....

....

....

....

....

....

....

....

....

....

My thoughts

SESSION 3

WHAT ABOUT PEOPLE WHO'VE NEVER HEARD ABOUT JESUS?

What makes you say, "That's not fair"?

All people are without excuse.

THE BIBLE MEETS LIFE

Unfairness hits all of us. Big issue or small, we want fairness. But unfairness rises to a new level when we're discussing eternal matters.

Is it "fair" for a loving God to punish an innocent person because he or she has never heard about Jesus Christ? This question arises from a faulty premise. The truth is no one is innocent. Everyone is guilty and deserves eternal separation from God (see Rom. 3:23; 5:12). Nevertheless, God in His mercy offered, through Jesus Christ, the way to be forgiven and receive eternal life. The Bible tells us:

1. God desires "everyone to be saved and to come to the knowledge of the truth" (1 Tim. 2:4).

2. Salvation is impossible apart from personal faith in Christ (see Acts 4:12).

How do we reconcile God's desire for all people to be saved with the fact that all people have not heard about Jesus Christ? Romans 1 provides valuable insight.

WHAT DOES THE BIBLE SAY?

Romans 1:16-25 *(HCSB)*

16 For I am not ashamed of the gospel, because it is God's power for salvation to everyone who believes, first to the Jew, and also to the Greek.

17 For in it God's righteousness is revealed from faith to faith, just as it is written: The righteous will live by faith.

18 For God's wrath is revealed from heaven against all godlessness and unrighteousness of people who by their unrighteousness suppress the truth,

19 since what can be known about God is evident among them, because God has shown it to them.

20 For His invisible attributes, that is, His eternal power and divine nature, have been clearly seen since the creation of the world, being understood through what He has made. As a result, people are without excuse.

21 For though they knew God, they did not glorify Him as God or show gratitude. Instead, their thinking became nonsense, and their senseless minds were darkened.

22 Claiming to be wise, they became fools

23 and exchanged the glory of the immortal God for images resembling mortal man, birds, four-footed animals, and reptiles.

24 Therefore God delivered them over in the cravings of their hearts to sexual impurity, so that their bodies were degraded among themselves.

25 They exchanged the truth of God for a lie, and worshiped and served something created instead of the Creator, who is praised forever. Amen.

Key Words

delivered them over (v. 24)—Expression used in a courtroom setting; a judge's order to carry out the sentence imposed on one found guilty of a crime.

salvation (v. 16)—Spiritual, eternal rescue God performs for those who trust Him through Jesus' work on the cross. Those who receive by faith Jesus' offer of salvation, God delivers from eternal damnation.

righteousness (v. 17)—Reflects both God's character of being just and His bringing people into right standing before Him. When used of people, it is often synonymous with salvation.

Romans 1:18-25

In our study of Psalm 19, we looked at two ways God has shown Himself to us.

▶ **General Revelation**: Information about God available to everyone through nature (such as God's power).

▶ **Special Revelation**: Information about God (such as the gospel of Jesus Christ) that is only available through the Bible.

In Romans 1:18-25 Paul details how some people have rejected the general revelation of God and therefore are without excuse before God. God has revealed Himself clearly. His "eternal power and divine nature" are clearly seen in His work of creation. All people are without excuse for rejecting God.

Verse 21 indicates that those who reject God "knew" Him but failed to honor Him or give Him thanks. This is an apt description of the essence of sin. We were created to enjoy fellowship with God and to dedicate our lives to glorifying Him. We have all fallen short of God's standard. Some who claimed to be wise became fools and proceeded to make a horrendous exchange. This exchange had God at its center. Fallen sinners become guilty of worshiping creation rather than the Creator.

Because of their shameless idolatry, God "delivered them over" to the impure desires of their hearts. God has removed His restraint so that sinful humans might experience the devastating consequences of their rebellion. The phrase "their bodies were degraded among themselves" is a reference to sexual sin. It is no coincidence that wherever we read of idolatry in Scripture, we find it accompanied by immorality.

Whether we are members of a pagan tribe in the isolated depths of another continent or managers of great wealth in a bustling city in America, the Bible declares us to be without excuse before the throne of a holy God. This is definitely bad news. But there is good news. The gospel of Jesus Christ offers hope to all of us who are without excuse.

What does it mean that people are without excuse?

QUESTION #1

Justice and Mercy International

> **Is it fair that people go to hell even though they have not heard about Jesus? Explain.**

"We should be astonished at the goodness of God, stunned that He should bother to call us by name."

—BRENNAN MANNING

POINTING TO **THE LIGHT**

☐ *Naturalism*

- Only the physical universe exists. Nothing supernatural exists.

- Human beings must create their own morality and purpose for life.

- Includes nihilism, existentialism, secular humanism, and atheism.

☐ *Animism*

- Some spirits live in material objects (like trees and rocks), while some are heavenly objects (like the sun and stars). Animals and people who have died may be viewed as deities.

- Humans help the spirits live in their world by making prayers and offerings. If they do well, the spirits provide humans with peace and prosperity.

- Includes witchcraft/wicca, astrology, fortune-telling, spiritism, and voodoo.

☐ *Far Eastern Thought*

- The essence of reality is not a personal god, but an impersonal life force.

- Pieces of the life force have spun away from its central core and are trying to work their way back. Every life form in the universe is a piece of that life force moving through successive lives (reincarnation) to higher and higher levels. Once it makes it to the highest level, the separated life force can then escape the material universe and merge back with the impersonal main body.

- Includes Hinduism, Buddhism, Hare Krishna, transcendental meditation, and some elements of the New Age movement.

Source: *Freddy Davis, www.MarketFaith.org*

Select one worldview. What in that worldview could I use to point people to Jesus Christ?

Romans 1:16-17

The fact that all of us are without excuse is a sobering reality, but let's remember what Paul wrote before he launched into the issue of our sinfulness: there is good news, and it is in the gospel of Jesus Christ!

The word "gospel" is synonymous with the concept of "good news." Paul boldly asserted that he was "not ashamed of the gospel." Paul was proud of the gospel because it is the very demonstration of God's power to save those who, left to themselves, are completely hopeless and under condemnation.

Paul communicated a very clear understanding of the gospel. How can a righteous God rescue those who have scorned Him and deserve His wrath without compromising His righteousness? The cross. God judged our sin in the death of His one and only Son. "But God proves His own love for us in that while we were still sinners, Christ died for us" (Rom. 5:8). God deals with our sin by allowing the judgment for our sins to fall on Christ.

At the same time God credits the righteousness of His Son to our account. Paul explained this amazing two-fold transaction this way: "He made the One who did not know sin to be sin for us, so that we might become the righteousness of God in Him" (2 Cor. 5:21).

In the gospel, the righteousness of God is revealed "from faith to faith." God reveals or activates His perfect plan of salvation "beginning and ending in faith." Biblical faith involves trust, reliance, and complete confidence in its object. I might intellectually believe an airplane is able to carry me safely to my desired destination, but not until I actually strap myself into my seat am I relying on that plane to transport me safely. Similarly, saving faith in Christ relies on the adequacy of Jesus to save us.

Sinful humans have access to the undeserved favor (grace) of God by faith. The gospel is the good news that Jesus brings salvation to all who place their faith in Him. Faith in Jesus is the way—the only way—to experience an abundant relationship with God that can begin now and extend throughout eternity.

How can we reconcile God's desire for all people to be saved with the fact that all people have not heard about Jesus?

QUESTION #3

What do verses 16-17 teach you about the heart of God?

QUESTION #4

LIVE IT OUT

So how do we respond to the questions regarding those who've never heard about Jesus?

▶ **Ask yourself**. Begin with your own response to the message of Christ. You have heard the Gospel, so respond with repentance and trust in Jesus Christ.

▶ **Get to know an unreached people group**. Research. Pray. Give. Ask God to reveal your role in reaching that people group.

▶ **Invest yourself in a mission experience**. Join a short-term mission trip with the goal of sharing Christ with an unreached group.

God could have devised any way to transmit the good news of Jesus Christ. He has chosen to entrust us with His message of reconciliation.

Men in the Grip of Ministry

Scott Lehman will never forget the day he used his seven iron to drive a golf ball through his sister's bedroom window. The most vivid part of the memory is not the sound of shattering glass, or hiding out in the old sand-filled John Deere® tractor tire, or even hearing his father shout his full name: "Scott Nelson Lehman! Where are you?" It was what his father said after brushing the sand off his tearful 10-year-old boy: "Son, you're forgiven."

To continue reading "Men in the Grip of Ministry" from *More Living* magazine, visit *BibleStudiesforLife.com/articles*.

My group's prayer requests

_____

_____

_____

_____

_____

_____

_____

_____

_____

_____

My thoughts

SESSION 4

WHY SHOULD I TRUST THE BIBLE?

What item from your childhood still works today?

The only safe place to build your life is on God's Word.

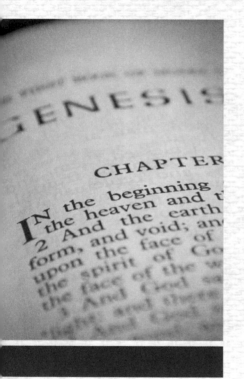

THE BIBLE MEETS LIFE

During this study we've seen the wonders of the universe argue for the existence of a Creator. But who is that Creator? Could the Creator be Allah of the Koran, "the Force" from Star Wars, or another deity people have worshiped throughout history?

The answer is found in the Bible. It points to God as the true and only Creator. Don't other religious books like the Koran of Islam and the Bhagavad Gita of Hinduism make similar claims? Why should we trust the Bible instead of other religious books to tell the truth about God?

Regardless of what product or item we consider dependable and reliable, it will fail us at sometime. Not so with the Bible.

Polls reveal, however, that an increasing number of people do not believe they can trust the Bible to be God's authoritative message. Nevertheless, despite its dismissal by skeptics, the Bible has been proven repeatedly to be trustworthy, reliable, and accurate. We're going to look into Psalm 119, a celebration of the character and impact of God's Word, which has the power to transform lives.

WHAT DOES THE BIBLE SAY?

Psalm 119:1-8,137-144 *(HCSB)*

1 How happy are those whose way is blameless, who live according to the LORD's instruction! **2** Happy are those who keep His decrees and seek Him with all their heart. **3** They do nothing wrong; they follow His ways. **4** You have commanded that Your precepts be diligently kept. **5** If only my ways were committed to keeping Your statutes! **6** Then I would not be ashamed when I think about all Your commands. **7** I will praise You with a sincere heart when I learn Your righteous judgments. **8** I will keep Your statutes; never abandon me.

137 You are righteous, LORD, and Your judgments are just. **138** The decrees You issue are righteous and altogether trustworthy. **139** My anger overwhelms me because my foes forget Your words. **140** Your word is completely pure, and Your servant loves it. **141** I am insignificant and despised, but I do not forget Your precepts. **142** Your righteousness is an everlasting righteousness, and Your instruction is true. **143** Trouble and distress have overtaken me, but Your commands are my delight. **144** Your decrees are righteous forever. Give me understanding, and I will live.

Key Words

judgments (v. 137)—Verdict in a court of law. Here it refers to God's decisions about right and wrong.

decrees (v. 138)—Covenant stipulations, often translated "testimony." God's decrees bear testimony to what is true.

precepts (v. 141)—A precept is a properly appointed principle, a mandate, a guideline for covenant living.

instruction (v. 142)—Also translated *Torah*, refers to a statute, the Ten Commandments, and even the first five books of the Bible.

Psalm 119:137-144

Psalm 119 is loaded with claims for the reliability and truthfulness of the Bible. We refer to this as internal evidence. Relying on claims the Bible makes about itself is circular reasoning (a method of false logic in which "A" is used to prove "B," and "B" is used to prove "A"). Many wonder if there is evidence outside of the Bible that confirms the trustworthiness of Scripture. Consider this external evidence.

▶ **Archaeology**. Archaeological discoveries have confirmed many locations and events in the Bible such as the location of Nineveh, the pool of Siloam (where Jesus healed the blind man),the Davidic dynasty, and the rule of Pontius Pilate. Archaeology has not disproved any event, person, or location in Scripture.

▶ **Multitude of manuscripts**. There are vast numbers of both Old and New Testament manuscripts, compared with the relatively few manuscripts of other works of antiquity. For example, the discovery of the Dead Sea Scrolls in 1947 included a nearly complete copy of the Book of Isaiah from 100 B.C., and demonstrated how accurately scribes had copied the text for almost a thousand years. The manuscript support for the New Testament is even more impressive. Today, there are more than 5,000 manuscripts of the Greek New Testament.

Contrast that to Homer's *Iliad*, which is next in terms of the number of available manuscripts. Only 643 ancient copies of *Iliad* are available, yet no one questions Homer's classic work. There is more—and earlier—manuscript support for the Jesus Christ described in the Gospels than for any other figure in the ancient world, including Julius Caesar and Alexander the Great.

▶ **The impact on humanity**. No book has changed the world more than the Bible. Kings and presidents, sailors and astronauts, and soldiers and peacemakers have invoked its words and articulated its principles. Many of us have read or heard stirring accounts that demonstrate the impact of the Bible.

Having addressed the issue of the Bible's reliability, we should ask ourselves the question,"If we believe it is reliable, are we relying on it as our guide for living?"

> *What are some reasons people question the reliability of the Bible?*

QUESTION #1

God intends for His Word to transform every aspect of our lives. As Psalm 119 so eloquently displays, God's Word is a treasure that illuminates the pathway to eternal life. Psalm 119:137-144 thunders forth the truth that God's Word is righteous, pure, and true. The writer used synonyms to refer to God:

▶ When the writer called the Lord "righteous" he was ascribing to Him a consistency of character in which there is no deviation.

▶ God is upright and maintains His own unswerving standard of perfection. Therefore, His rules or judgments are altogether right, since His rules reflect His character.

▶ The Lord's everlasting righteousness expresses itself in a law that is true. All that God has spoken is accurate and devoid of even the slightest taint of falsehood.

For this reason the psalmist called the Lord's commandments his delight. Certainly the psalmist was acquainted at times with trouble and anguish. The righteous, pure, and true Word of the Lord sustained and nourished him in times of distress.

In verse 144 the writer repeats his assertion of verse 142. God's Word is righteous forever. One constant of human existence is change. God's Word, however, is unchanging. It will never be less righteous, pure, or true than it is now or has been in the past. This is the case because God's Word reflects His character (see Heb. 13:8).

> *What do these verses teach us about God and His Word?*
>
> QUESTION #2

RELIABLE DIRECTION

What is a source of advice people look to on these topics?

Work/Career	Marriage	Finances
....	....	....

Raising Kids	Cooking	Other
....	....	....

How the Bible has proven reliable to me:

Psalm 119:1-8

Let's move to the front of the psalm and consider what happens to us when we follow God's Word. We are blessed. This happiness and blessedness is independent of circumstances. It is rooted in confidence that God produces contentment in all circumstances, good or bad.

Happy and blessed is the state of those who value God above all things. It is also the state of those who experience firsthand the joy that flows from conformity to God's Word.

The psalmist began by blessing those whose ways are blameless. These people live consistent with God's principles. Certainly, the psalmist was not sinless, and neither are we. But, like him, we aim for growing in conformity to God's Word rather than simply being satisfied with our current state.

The psalmist was determined not just to know God's Word, but to order his life by it. How do we grow in obedience and avoid what is wrong? The answer is to learn to walk—to live—in the ways of the Lord. This requires intense and diligent effort on our part. This effort is not an attempt to earn favor with God but, rather, it is a response to His gracious revelation of Himself.

According to verse 6, those whose eyes are fixed—or concentrated—on all of the Lord's commandments will not be put to shame. Others may mistreat them, but the God who knows all things and honors commitment to His Word will sustain them through it all. Verse 7 makes the very powerful correlation between knowing God's Word and honoring Him with praise. As we grow in our knowledge of God's Word, we find more and more reasons to praise Him.

Finally, in verse 8, we see the psalmist's resolve and determination to keep the Lord's statutes and to obey His Word. His request to not be utterly forsaken is acknowledgement of his desperate need for divine help and restraint as he strives to live according to God's commands.

When have you seen the Bible's instruction work?

QUESTION #3

Why do we follow God's Word?

QUESTION #4

LIVE IT OUT

When the writer called the Lord "righteous," he ascribed to Him a consistency of character in which there is no deviation. How can you build your life on this altogether right God? For starters:

▶ **Schedule time to read God's Word**. To discover how God blesses, start with Proverbs and read a chapter each day for a month. Do at least one of the proverbs that very day.

▶ **Dig deeper**. Read chapter 2, "How Can I Know the Bible is True?" in *How Can I Know?* by Robert Jeffress. Invite others to read and discuss it with you.

▶ **Disciple a new believer**. Coach someone else in developing a lifelong habit of Bible reading and study.

Psalm 119 calls us to move from abstract generalities to concrete realities about the Bible. Honoring the God of the Bible means personalizing and applying His commands.

On the Same Page

Though my husband, Anwar, and I both love God's Word, all attempts to consistently explore it together had failed rather miserably. We were both growing, though we rarely found ourselves, quite literally, on the same page. I longed for the oneness described in Genesis 2, where Adam and Eve "became one flesh." How could that mystery translate to this portion of our relationship?

To continue reading "On the Same Page" from *HomeLife* magazine, visit *BibleStudiesforLife.com/articles*.

My group's prayer requests

....
....
....
....
....
....
....
....
....
....
....

My thoughts

SESSION 5

HOW DID WE GET HERE AND WHY?

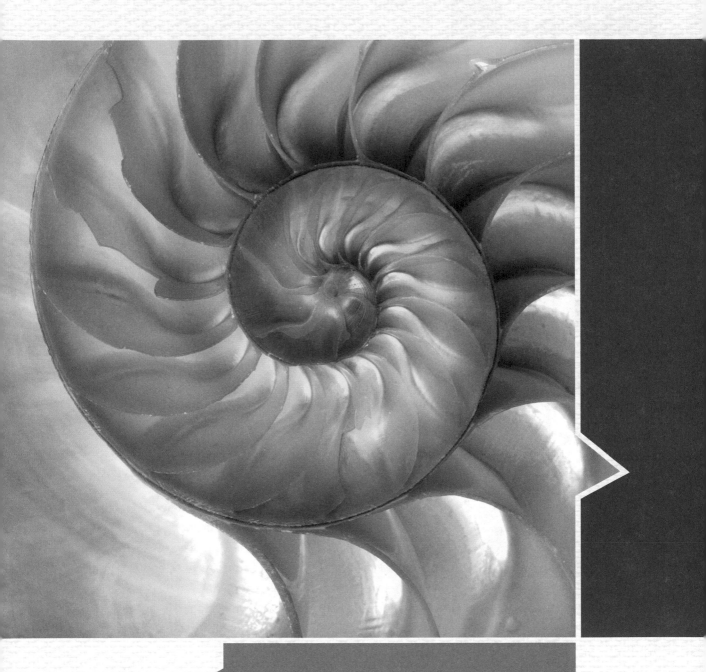

In all creation, what is most intriguing to you?

The universe is here because God spoke.

THE BIBLE MEETS LIFE

The world around us is so full of fascinating and intriguing things. We have not even scratched the surface of understanding all the marvels of the universe. At the University of Cambridge, the physics laboratory (called the Cavendish Laboratory) has the words of Psalm 111:2 inscribed over the entrance to its building: "The works of the LORD are great, sought out of all them that have pleasure therein" (KJV).

Science and faith are not opposed to one another. Many scientists do not separate God from science; they see God behind the science.

When you look at the wonders of the universe, what does it tell you about how it all came to be? How we view the origins of the universe influences everything else about our worldview. Did everything come to exist merely by chance, or is the universe and everything in it the creative work of an intelligent Being? The Bible points us to an all-powerful and personal Creator who was and is responsible for everything in the universe, which He spoke into existence.

WHAT DOES THE BIBLE SAY?

Genesis 1:1-3,6,9,11,14,20,26-27 *(HCSB)*

1 In the beginning God created the heavens and the earth. **2** Now the earth was formless and empty, darkness covered the surface of the watery depths, and the Spirit of God was hovering over the surface of the waters. **3** Then God said, "Let there be light," and there was light.

....

6 Then God said, "Let there be an expanse between the waters, separating water from water."

....

9 Then God said, "Let the water under the sky be gathered into one place, and let the dry land appear." And it was so.

....

11 Then God said, "Let the earth produce vegetation: seed-bearing plants and fruit trees on the earth bearing fruit with seed in it according to their kinds." And it was so.

....

14 Then God said, "Let there be lights in the expanse of the sky to separate the day from the night. They will serve as signs for festivals and for days and years.

....

20 Then God said, "Let the water swarm with living creatures, and let birds fly above the earth across the expanse of the sky."

....

26 Then God said, "Let Us make man in Our image, according to Our likeness. They will rule the fish of the sea, the birds of the sky, the livestock, all the earth, and the creatures that crawl on the earth." **27** So God created man in His own image; He created him in the image of God; He created them male and female.

Key Words

formless and empty (v. 2)— Could be translated "shapeless" and "void." There was neither shape nor content.

image (v. 26)—How humans are like God. Genesis does not specify details. Bible students suggest it refers to our spiritual nature, moral capacity, reasoning ability, immortality, and so forth.

Genesis 1:1-3,6,9,11,14,20

In John 1:1-3 John echoes the truth of God's creative power that Genesis 1 describes in detail. As we understand creation, we more easily understand other Bible teachings such as the fall of man, which necessitated that Jesus Christ die for sin. What you believe about creation determines what you believe about humanity. Your view of humanity reveals what you believe about sin. What you believe about sin shapes what you believe about our Savior Jesus Christ. God did not leave us with the option of choosing what parts of Scripture to believe. The Bible's testimony is six-day creation and third-day resurrection.

There are three basic views of the origin of the cosmos.

1. An all-powerful God spoke everything into existence.

2. There was nothing and then there was something. It just happened.

3. Matter has always existed and is eternal. At a point in time, matter randomly became organized.

God created *ex nihilo*—out of nothing. Theistic evolution has been rightly labeled as a theological disaster and an untenable position. God spoke the universe into existence. At least nine times in Genesis 1, you will find, "God said." These two words emphasize God's awesome power. He has the ability to command nothing to become something. Many people are creative. The difference between their creations and God's is they create things out of material that already exists. God created the universe out of what did not exist. Nothing exists in creation that God did not first call into being. Scholars frequently use *ex nihilo* to describe God's work of creating without pre-existing material. This staggers our finite minds and reflects the incomparable power of God.

> *Why does it matter what we believe about the origins of the universe?*
>
> QUESTION #1

Note the purpose given for each element. God's work in creation is purposeful, not haphazard. We see:

▶ The priority of God as the Author, Source, and Cause of creation.

▶ The miraculous manner of His creative work as He speaks things into existence.

▶ The scope of His creative work that encompasses "the heavens and the earth."

Day 1. The first day marks the creation of light. God evaluated the light as "good" and named the light "day" and the darkness "night." His act of naming signifies His ownership of creation.

Day 2. The Lord made a division between the waters and the atmospheric heaven. Notice the statement of fulfillment in verse 7: "And it was so."

Day 3. We see increasing movement from formlessness to fullness. God set boundaries for seas and provided for dry land (v. 9). He called the earth to produce vegetation (plants, trees) to bear seeds and fruit (v. 11).

Day 4. On the fourth day came God's purposeful creation of the sun, moon, and stars—lights to regulate day and night, times, and seasons.

Day 5. God created life in the seas and skies. Then He pronounced the first recorded blessing in the Bible when He blessed these creatures with a command to be fruitful and multiply.

> *What can we learn about our Creator from the opening verses of the Bible?*
>
> QUESTION **#2**

Genesis 1:26-27

All of God's work up to this point was simply a prelude to His ultimate act of creation on the sixth day. What is unique about the creation of the first man and woman is God created them in His own image and likeness. God fashioned the human with attributes that reflect His own nature—attributes that would enable him to have a relationship with God. The human was made with the capacity:

▶ To know God

▶ To have a relationship with Him

▶ To represent His interests on the earth

God created human beings to have dominion over all the earth, to procreate, to labor, and to steward His resources. Before the fall described in Genesis 3, humans—male and female—existed as the image bearers of God, untouched by the devastating disease of sin.

The Bible repeatedly emphasizes that the God who created us in His image created us male and female. There are no generic human beings. We are either male or female. This carries enormous implications for marriages and families.

The uniqueness and sanctity of human life may be traced back to the reality that God made us in His image. People are not the product of fate or chance. We are the result of the purposeful, creative power of a holy God. Being made in God's image brings with it inestimable privilege and distinct responsibility.

The image of God in us has been marred, leading us to pursue our own purpose rather than the purpose for which God designed us. But in redemption through Jesus Christ, God's purpose for us is restored. Lasting peace and true realization of our purpose comes from being rightly related to the God who created us.

> *What feelings are stirred up when you read that you are made in the image of God?*
>
> QUESTION #3

> *How does the fact that we are God's image bearers influence what we say and do?*
>
> QUESTION #4

CREATED WITH **PURPOSE**

FACT:	HOW THIS FACT IMPACTS:

WHAT I DO MATTERS

My Home:

My Church:

My Community:

LIVE IT OUT

The Bible points us to an all-powerful and personal Creator. How does this reality influence your life?

▶ **Trust God with your circumstances**. Since God can speak a universe into existence, He can be trusted with your life.

▶ **See people as God sees them**. Just as you are created in God's image, so is everyone else. Lead someone to discover the value God has placed on him or her.

▶ **Value God's creation**. We don't worship nature, but identify ways you can care for God's creation.

You are created in the image of the God of the universe. Let that truth influence your words and motives.

A Deeper Shade of Green

Green is the new black. Environmental awareness is trendy, cool, in vogue. What was once reserved for Birkenstock-wearing flower children is cruising into the mainstream like a speeding Prius. Fashion is green. Outdoor-wear company Patagonia produces fleece jackets made from recycled plastic bottles. Even Sam's Club now sells jeans and T-shirts made with organic cotton, making Walmart the largest purchaser of organic cotton in the world as of 2006.

To continue reading "A Deeper Shade of Green" from *HomeLife* magazine, visit *BibleStudiesforLife.com/articles*.

My group's prayer requests

....

....

....

....

....

....

....

....

....

My thoughts

SESSION 6

IF GOD IS GOOD, WHY IS THERE SUFFERING?

What makes life better
when you feel lousy?

> *God meets us in our suffering.*

THE BIBLE MEETS LIFE

"Why, God?"

Since the beginning of time people have asked "why" in the midst of suffering. Author Lee Strobel cites a national survey that asked, "If you could ask God one question and knew He would answer, what would it be?" The top response? "Why is there pain and suffering in the world?"*

Skeptics often cite the reality of suffering as evidence against the biblical view of God. After all, if God is loving but does not stop evil and suffering, then He must not be all-powerful. Skeptics say the only alternative is that God is able to prevent evil and suffering and does not do so, which means He does not love.

The Bible assures us God is both loving and all-powerful despite the suffering and evil that are part of life. Although we cannot always answer the "why" question about suffering in general—or every individual example in particular—we can know that God loves us.

* Lee Strobel, *The Case for Faith* (Zondervan, 2000)

WHAT DOES THE BIBLE SAY?

Job 30:26-31; 42:1-6 *(HCSB)*

30:26 But when I hoped for good, evil came; when I looked for light, darkness came.

27 I am churning within and cannot rest; days of suffering confront me.

28 I walk about blackened, but not by the sun. I stood in the assembly and cried out for help.

29 I have become a brother to jackals and a companion of ostriches.

30 My skin blackens and flakes off, and my bones burn with fever.

31 My lyre is used for mourning and my flute for the sound of weeping.

42:1 Then Job replied to the LORD:

2 I know that You can do anything and no plan of Yours can be thwarted.

3 You asked, "Who is this who conceals My counsel with ignorance?" Surely I spoke about things I did not understand, things too wonderful for me to know.

4 You said, "Listen now, and I will speak. When I question you, you will inform Me."

5 I had heard rumors about You, but now my eyes have seen You.

6 Therefore I take back my words and repent in dust and ashes.

Key Words

no plan of Yours can be thwarted (v. 2)—When God decides to do something, nothing and no one can stop Him, for He created everything and everyone.

repent in dust and ashes (v. 6)—The ancients recognized sitting in dust and ashes as a sign of repentance, contrition, or deep sorrow.

Job 30:26-31

God allowed Satan to afflict Job with intense suffering that included the loss of family, possessions, and health. Job cherished God more than these things, and he ultimately chose to trust in God's sovereignty and love. However, such faith did not come easily or instantly.

▶ His longings for good and light were seemingly mocked by evil and darkness (v. 26).

▶ He faced inner turmoil (v. 27).

▶ His skin was blackened and flaking off—likely by some dreadful disease (vv. 28,30).

▶ He cried out in desperation like the howl of a wild animal (vv. 28-29).

▶ The glad music of his life had turned into woeful mourning (v. 31).

What does this picture of Job's suffering teach us?

1. All people experience suffering. Commitment to God and consistency of character don't exempt anyone from pain in this life.

2. Our suffering is not always the direct result of our personal sin. Suffering is a by-product of living in a world corrupted by sin. Sometimes the evil we experience is the result of others' sins.

> **What is it we question about God when we read these verses?**
>
> QUESTION #1

Job was a man seeking to honor the Lord. Why, then, did he suffer? Why did God grant Satan even limited power to inflict intense pain on one of God's choicest servants? While we don't know all the answers to such questions, we can make inferences. One is that God's power and sufficiency are highlighted against the backdrop of our weakness and suffering (see 2 Cor. 12:7-10). When you comprehend how far we have fallen short of God's desires for us, the ultimate question may change from "Why do we suffer?" to "Why don't we suffer more?"

WHAT DO I DO?

Based on Job, what do I say or do?

A neighbor suffers from chronic migraine headaches.

....
....

A friend was down-sized and can't seem to land a job because of his age.

....
....

Your niece is a paraplegic due to a hit-and-run accident.

....
....

"However deep the pit,
God's love is deeper still."

—CORRIE TEN BOOM

Job 42:1-3

Job 42 is Job's response to God's speech recorded in chapters 38–41. Job's speech reminds us that while we don't know the precise reasons for our suffering, we can be assured of God's power and knowledge.

God's questioning of Job in chapter 38 highlights the distinction between finite man and the infinite God. When we are ambushed by adversity, it is normal and acceptable to ask God questions and to tell Him we don't understand. However, it is never right for finite creatures to question the integrity of God.

Consider just two of the questions God posed in Job 38.

▶ Where was Job when God laid the foundations of the earth?

▶ Who "enclosed the sea behind doors," meaning who placed limits on the waves and the tides?

With questions God illustrated the vast difference between a timeless God and a time-bound person. God's wisdom makes so-called human wisdom look like ignorance. Job willingly admitted that he had obscured knowledge by speaking of things he didn't understand, that were "too wonderful" for him.

George Müller, known for his work with orphans in England during the 19th century, has left a legacy of confidence in God. Speaking at his wife's funeral after 39 years of marriage, Müller said: "I seek by perfect submission to His holy will to glorify Him. I kiss continually the hand that has thus afflicted me." While we may never fully grasp the reasons for suffering, we can know God understands and cares.

> *What has caused you to question God's wisdom or power?*

QUESTION **#2**

Job 42:4-6

Job extended his confession to include repentance. Suffering should draw us closer to God, rather than drive us away. Job repented of questioning God's goodness. After God spoke in chapters 38–41, Job was armed with a new awareness of God's character. He was sensitized to the seriousness of his error.

Not only did Job repudiate his earlier, flawed beliefs about God, but he also repented of them. Verse 6 gives us a picture of biblical repentance which involves a radical change in direction and perspective. The reference to "dust and ashes" indicates that Job adopted a genuine posture of humility. We find comfort and relief in acknowledging that we don't have all the answers, as we bow humbly before the One who does.

We have a God who comprehends our pain because He has experienced every kind of hardship we encounter. Jesus Christ understands what it is like to be betrayed by a friend, misunderstood by family members, falsely accused by enemies, and even to feel forsaken by our Heavenly Father. That is why we can talk confidently to God when we are suffering, certain that He empathizes with our situation. "For we do not have a high priest who is unable to sympathize with our weaknesses, but One who has been tested in every way as we are, yet without sin. Therefore let us approach the throne of grace with boldness, so that we may receive mercy and find grace to help us at the proper time" (Heb. 4:15-16).

Job's story concludes as he repents and is given a renewed understanding of God's sovereign power and goodness. Suffering can and should be a catalyst that drives us deeper into the strong and loving arms of the Father who loved us enough to sacrifice His One and Only Son for us.

> **What can we do to express faith in the midst of suffering?**

QUESTION #4

LIVE IT OUT

Determine to meet suffering armed with God's love and presence, "casting all your care on Him, because He cares about you" (1 Pet. 5:7). Three of many ways to do this:

▶ **Refuse despair**. It's OK to grieve, but that doesn't mean we have to despair. Trust God's love and goodness.

▶ **Be there**. You often don't have to say a word, but your presence can be a great comfort to those suffering.

▶ **Help**. Connect with a friend or two to minister to families suffering through illness, hospitalization, or the death of a loved one. Develop a list of needs, and enlist other volunteers to help meet these needs as long as necessary.

God loves you and will meet you in your suffering.

A Shoulder to Lean On

Lacking confidence for the right words, people often shy away from parents in the midst of receiving a special needs diagnosis. After interviewing a number of mothers of children affected by special needs, common pointers emerge to help caring friends better engage these families.

To continue reading "A Shoulder to Lean On" from *ParentLife* magazine, visit *BibleStudiesforLife.com/articles*.

My group's prayer requests

My thoughts

Honest to God: Real Questions People Ask

We have discussed some difficult questions in this study. Our goal has been two-fold. First, discussing these tough questions from the Bible's perspective helps us speak graciously and knowingly with those who question our beliefs. Second, this study helps us gain a solid footing for our own beliefs. We don't have to simply believe something "blindly"; we can say confidently what we believe and why we believe it.

Christus

Belief in Jesus does not have to be a blind faith. Tackling the tough questions can actually strengthen one's belief in Christ. Those who question the nature and character of God need only to look at what God has done through Christ to see He is trustworthy, good, and loving.

Community

These tough questions are more than just an academic exercise. The circumstances of life can often lead believers to experience some of these very questions. When fellow believers begin to question the goodness or love of God because of some turn of events, we can confidently and encouragingly stand with them.

Culture

Our culture has moved from assuming Christian beliefs to ignoring those beliefs and now to challenging or rejecting those beliefs. Christians do not need to go off into a corner; we can stand up to the skepticism and questioning of culture. With love, graciousness, and solid reasoning we can give people a reason to follow Jesus Christ.

GENERAL INSTRUCTIONS

In order to make the most of this study and to ensure a richer group experience, it's recommended that all group participants read through the teaching and discussion content in full before each group meeting. As a leader, it is also a good idea for you to be familiar with this content and prepared to summarize it for your group members as you move through the material each week.

Each session of the Bible study is made up of three sections:

1. THE BIBLE MEETS LIFE.

An introduction to the theme of the session and its connection to everyday life, along with a brief overview of the primary Scripture text. This section also includes an icebreaker question or activity.

2. WHAT DOES THE BIBLE SAY?

This comprises the bulk of each session and includes the primary Scripture text along with explanations for key words and ideas within that text. This section also includes most of the content designed to produce and maintain discussion within the group.

3. LIVE IT OUT.

The final section focuses on application, using bulleted summary statements to answer the question, *So what?* As the leader, be prepared to challenge the group to apply what they learned during the discussion by transforming it into action throughout the week.

For group leaders, the *Honest to God* Leader Guide contains several features and tools designed to help you lead participants through the material provided.

ICEBREAKER

These opening questions and/or activities are designed to help participants transition into the study and begin engaging the primary themes to be discussed. Be sure everyone has a chance to speak, but maintain a low-pressure environment.

DISCUSSION QUESTIONS

Each "What Does the Bible Say?" section features at least three questions designed to spark discussion and interaction within your group. These questions encourage critical thinking, so be sure to allow a period of silence for participants to process the question and form an answer.

The *Honest to God* Leader Guide also contains follow-up questions and optional activities that may be helpful to your group, if time permits.

DVD CONTENT

Each video features teaching from Robert Jeffress on the primary themes found in the session. We recommend that you show this video in one of three places: (1) At the beginning of group time, (2) After the icebreaker, or (3) After a quick review and/or summary of "What Does the Bible Say?" A video summary is included as well. You may choose to use this summary as background preparation to help you guide the group.

The Leader Guide contains additional questions to help unpack the video and transition into the discussion.

Note: For more biblical depth on these topics, be sure to *review the commentary* provided in the "Leader Tools" folder on the DVD-ROM in your Leader Kit. A digital Leader Guide is also included.

SESSION ONE: IS EVERY LIFE SACRED?

The Point: God values life and so should we.

The Passage: Psalm 139:1-6,13-18

The Setting: Psalm 139 is a very personal Psalm. David wrote of God's incomparable attributes—His omniscience, omnipotence, and omnipresence—but he wrote of those attributes in the context of how God knew him and was personally involved in the details of his life.

Icebreaker: How can people tell what is valuable to you?

> *Optional activity:* Bring to the group meeting several pictures and/or descriptions of items for sale, ranging from inexpensive to expensive. Cover the prices of each item beforehand. During the group meeting, pass the item descriptions around one at a time and encourage participants to guess the retail price for each one. When everyone has made their guess for an item, reveal the actual cost.
>
> Once all the items have been discussed, conclude with the following questions:
>
> - How do stores and retail establishments calculate the value of their products?
>
> - How does our society calculate the value of people?

Video Summary: In this video session, Robert talks about the sacred nature of life. He explains that *sacred* means to be set apart. God has set apart our lives for a special purpose. Psalm 139 illustrates how God knows us. God not only knows *about* us, He desires to have a relationship *with* us. Psalm 139:13 says, "It was You who created my inward parts; You knit me together in my mother's womb." Every part of us has been designed by God. He made us just the way we are. And He has a special purpose and relationship in mind for us.

WATCH THE DVD SEGMENT FOR SESSION 1, THEN USE THE FOLLOWING QUESTIONS AND DISCUSSION POINTS TO TRANSITION INTO THE STUDY.

- In Exodus 4:10, Moses tells God, "I am slow and hesitant in speech." But this didn't change God's plan for Moses. Instead, it was part of His plan to glorify Himself through Moses. What obstacle in your life have you seen God use for His glory?

- Robert also talks about Christians living out the message that all life—inside and outside the womb—is sacred. That seems like an enormous undertaking. It's hard to know where to even start. What are some things you could do to make an impact?

WHAT DOES THE BIBLE SAY?

ASK FOR A VOLUNTEER TO READ ALOUD PSALM 139:1-6,13-18.

Response: What's your initial reaction to these verses?

- What do you like about the text?

- What questions do you have about these verses?

TURN THE GROUP'S ATTENTION TO PSALM 139:1-6.

QUESTION 1: From these verses, how can you know that God values you?

This is an observation question that requires the group to consider how intimately God knows them. Encourage group members to examine closely Psalm 139:1-6.

Optional follow-up: What emotions do you experience when you read these verses? Why?

Optional activity: Direct group members to the activity labeled "Expressing Value" on p. 9. Ask for volunteers to share their responses.

MOVE TO PSALM 139:13-16.

QUESTION 2: Since life begins at conception, how does this impact our attitudes toward the hardest questions about abortion?

The focus here is that God knows us at the moment of conception. You may steer the discussion more toward how this impacts the abortion issue as it relates to conception and how the Bible defines where life begins.

QUESTION 3: What should characterize our treatment of others (the sick, poor, disabled, elderly) in light of the fact that we are all fearfully and wonderfully made?

This question is ultimately about application. Specifically, how does the group "apply" the fact that we are fearfully and wonderfully made? You may establish context by first asking the group what it means to be fearfully and wonderfully made.

Optional follow-up: Why is God worthy of our praise because we are fearfully and wonderfully made?

Optional follow-up: In what ways do you intentionally express praise to God, as the psalmist did?

CONTINUE WITH PSALM 139:17-18.

QUESTION 4: Which attribute of God mentioned in these verses have you recently seen firsthand?

The attribute being described here is how God, with thoughts as numerous as there are grains of sand, still keeps us in mind constantly. Challenge the group to answer with ways they have experienced this aspect of God.

Note: The following question does not appear in the group member book. Use it in your group discussion as time allows.

QUESTION 5: How can we actively and intentionally choose to value life in our everyday routines?

This is an application question included to move members toward definitive action.

Optional follow-up: Based on the actions mentioned in response to question 5, what specific steps can you take this week to bring these things about? Refer to the Live It Out section for ideas if needed.

LIVE IT OUT

Psalm 139 shows that God values human life. Direct group members to three ways they can do the same.

- **Write a letter that values life.** Perhaps you'll enclose money to help save babies and enhance lives. Your local school might need a piece of playground equipment that accommodates a child who happens to be in a wheelchair.

- **Show grace.** Many people suffer silently with guilt over involvement with a past abortion. If you know someone like this, extend God's love and grace to him or her.

- **Form a friendship with someone who's been labeled.** Think about the descriptors "homeless," "terminally ill," "mentally handicapped," and so on. Getting to know someone will change your attitude about that person.

Challenge: Whom do you know who has been abused, hurt, neglected, disrespected, or otherwise marginalized? Seek out one of those people this week and invest in him or her. If you have personally experienced any of these things, consider using your story to help strengthen the life and faith of one who is still in the midst of the struggle.

Pray: Ask for prayer requests and ask group members to pray for the different requests as intercessors. As the leader, close this time by committing the members of your group to the Lord and asking Him to help each of you value life as He does.

SESSION TWO: HOW CAN I BE SURE GOD EXISTS?

The Point: God has given us ways to know Him.

The Passage: Psalm 19:1-14

The Setting: Psalm 19 declares the glory and majesty of God has been made clear to us in two ways. First, God has revealed Himself in a general way through creation (vv. 1-6). All people can know of God because His creation points to His existence and attributes. Second, God has specifically revealed Himself through Scripture (vv. 7-14).

Icebreaker: What architecture, music, or marvel moves you?

> *Optional activity:* Set up a laptop or tablet so that participants can search for images and/or samples in order to demonstrate their answers to the icebreaker question.

Video Summary: The Scripture passage for this week starts with, "The heavens declare the glory of God, and the sky proclaims the work of His hands" (Psalm 19:1). This week Robert talks about how the issue is not whether we can prove or disprove God exists. It's a matter of what the evidence shows and whether the evidence argues for or against the existence of God. God is a personal Creator who desires a relationship with us. And when a person truly desires to know God, He will do everything necessary to reveal Himself through Jesus Christ.

WATCH THE DVD SEGMENT FOR SESSION 2, THEN USE THE FOLLOWING QUESTIONS AND DISCUSSION POINTS TO TRANSITION INTO THE STUDY.

- Robert talks about how it has become more acceptable in our culture to voice our doubts and disbeliefs. What examples of this have you encountered?

- God has gone to great lengths for us to know Him. How does this knowledge impact how you make a case for His existence with others?

WHAT DOES THE BIBLE SAY?

ASK FOR A VOLUNTEER TO READ ALOUD PSALM 19:1-14.
Response: What's your initial reaction to these verses?

- What questions do you have about these verses?

- What do you hope to gain from this passage about being sure that God exists?

TURN THE GROUP'S ATTENTION TO PSALM 19:1-6.
QUESTION 1: Creation can tell us about God's eminence (His dominion over creation), but what can it tell us about His imminence (His nearness)?

This question asks group members to interpret this passage as it relates to God's "nearness." It's easy for most of us to see God as far removed, but it can be challenging to understand His imminence.

> *Optional follow-up:* In what ways have you experienced the imminence of God?

QUESTION 2: If nature reveals God so clearly, why do we sometimes struggle to believe?

This question is self-revelatory in nature. It asks us to examine more closely the obstacles we encounter in faith.

> *Optional follow-up:* When have you experienced God or felt close to Him while interacting with nature?

MOVE TO PSALM 19:7-11.
QUESTION 3: What does the Bible reveal about God that nature does not?

This question is included to help the group understand that knowledge of God is never-ending. It's infinite. Although we can learn about God through nature, we can never learn all there is to know.

> *Optional follow-up:* How do God's general revelation and special revelation complement each other?

CONTINUE WITH PSALM 19:12-14.
QUESTION 4: How does the existence of God impact the way you approach each day?

This application question is predicated on God's existence. In terms of the ways God has given us to know Him, this question asks the group to reflect on how they live out their knowledge of God.

> *Optional activity:* Direct group members to the activity labeled "Nurturing Faith" on p. 21. Ask for volunteers to share their responses to one of the three options.

Note: The following question does not appear in the group member book. Use it in your group discussion as time allows.

QUESTION 5: How can we use general revelation and special revelation to help others come to a knowledge of God?

This question is about taking all forms of revelation and using them to help others know God.

LIVE IT OUT

God has provided us with powerful clues, in nature and in His Word, about His existence and greatness. Encourage group members to review these three ways to respond to His revelation.

- **Look around.** Look up at the sky or at nature around you. What do you see that indicates God is real?

- **Join the chorus.** Seek to live your life so that it joins creation in declaring the glory of God. Let your actions point to God.

- **Express your faith.** Explain to someone why you believe God is real based on both nature and Scripture. When you put your convictions into words, you grasp better the truth you hold inwardly.

Challenge: Read Psalm 19:7-11 several times this week to remind yourself why you want to listen to God's words.

Pray: Ask for prayer requests and ask group members to pray for the different requests as intercessors. As the leader, close this time by committing the members of your group to the Lord and asking Him to help each of you embrace a true relationship with Him and build your lives around Him.

SESSION THREE: WHAT ABOUT PEOPLE WHO'VE NEVER HEARD ABOUT JESUS?

The Point: All people are without excuse.

The Passage: Romans 1:16-25

The Setting: The Book of Romans is Paul's orderly explanation of the gospel. Romans could be described as a treatise on the doctrine of salvation. He began by showing that all of us are in need of this salvation because we are all sinners. None of us is without excuse, for even the world around us points us to God.

Icebreaker: What makes you say, "That's not fair"?

Optional follow-up: What emotions do you experience when you're accused of being unfair?

Optional activity: Ask for pairs of volunteers to role-play the situations described below. In each situation, one person is identified as acting fairly while the other person will act unfairly. Go through as many situations as time allows.

- An employee (fair) is asking his or her boss (unfair) for a raise.

- A teenager (unfair) is demanding from his or her parent (fair) the right to attend a party.

- A homeowner (fair) is confronting his or her neighbor (unfair) about a fence that illegally crosses property lines.

Video Summary: God loves us so much that whenever He sees someone who truly wants to know Him, He'll send the gospel. In his video message, Robert gives two examples of this—the Ethiopian eunuch (see Acts 8) and Cornelius (see Acts 10). "The Lord does not delay His promise, as some understand delay, but is patient with you, not wanting any to perish but all to come to repentance" (2 Peter 3:9). God isn't trying to condemn as many people as possible, He is trying to save as many people as possible. Knowledge of God is available to everyone. "It is God's power for salvation to everyone who believes, first to the Jew, and also to the Greek" (Romans 1:16).

WATCH THE DVD SEGMENT FOR SESSION 3, THEN USE THE FOLLOWING QUESTIONS AND DISCUSSION POINTS TO TRANSITION INTO THE STUDY.

- God not only ordained the end, but He ordained the means to the end. And that means is us. Who has been instrumental in making sure you know about Jesus?

- What do you see as your responsibility in making sure others know about Jesus?

WHAT DOES THE BIBLE SAY?

ASK FOR A VOLUNTEER TO READ ALOUD ROMANS 1:16-25.
Response: What's your initial reaction to these verses?

- What questions do you have about these verses?

- What new application do you hope to get from this passage?

TURN THE GROUP'S ATTENTION TO ROMANS 1:18-25.
QUESTION 1: What does it mean that people are without excuse?

This is an observation question included as a means for group discussion of the point for this session: All people are without excuse.

Optional follow-up: What are some situations in which people are "without excuse" in everyday life?

QUESTION 2: Is it fair that people go to hell even though they have not heard about Jesus? Explain.

This question has been included to reinforce the fact that we are without excuse. You may stress that this paradigm is not about fairness as much as it is about biblical truth. In "fairness" all people have equal access to the salvation that Jesus offers.

Optional follow-up: What emotions have you experienced so far during this discussion? Why?

Optional activity: Direct group members to the activity labeled "Pointing to the Light" on p. 30. Ask for volunteers to share their response regarding one of the worldviews mentioned.

MOVE TO ROMANS 1:16-17.
QUESTION 3: How can we reconcile God's desire for all people to be saved with the fact that all people have not heard about Jesus?

Philippians 2:12 encourages us to work out our salvation with fear and trembling. Try to help group members work through the tension present in this question in order to strengthen convictions.

QUESTION 4: What do verses 16-17 teach you about the heart of God?

This observation question points the group to the specific verses in the text.

> *Optional follow-up:* How does the concept of faith apply to our discussion?

Note: The following question does not appear in the group member book. Use it in your group discussion as time allows.

QUESTION 5: What questions or tensions from this discussion feel unresolved to you?

This is an opportunity for the group to put a touch of finality on the discussion.

> *Optional follow-up:* How can you move forward in your walk with God even if these questions or tensions remain unresolved?

LIVE IT OUT

So how do we respond to the questions regarding those who have never heard about Jesus? Explain to group members that the best answer we can give from this passage is that God will deal with each person based on what they do with the revelation of who God is and what Jesus Christ has done.

- **Ask yourself.** Begin with your own response to the message of Christ. You have heard the Gospel, so respond with repentance and trust in Jesus Christ.

- **Get to know an unreached people group.** Research. Pray. Give. Ask God to reveal your role in reaching that people group.

- **Invest yourself in a mission experience.** Join a short-term mission trip with a goal of sharing Christ with an unreached group.

Challenge: Be mindful of the times you question the fairness of situations this week. Instead of asking, "Is it fair?" try replacing that with, "How can I help?" God could have chosen any way to transmit the good news of Jesus, but He has entrusted His message to us.

Pray: Ask for prayer requests and ask group members to pray for the different requests as intercessors. As the leader, close this time by asking the Lord to help each of you do your part in making sure those who've never heard the good news of Jesus Christ hear this message soon.

SESSION FOUR: WHY SHOULD I TRUST THE BIBLE?

The Point: The only safe place to build your life is on God's Word.

The Passage: Psalm 119:1-8,137-144

The Setting: Psalm 119 is not only the longest Psalm, but it is longer than 30 entire books in the Bible. It is comprised of 22 stanzas, and each stanza begins with a successive letter of the Hebrew alphabet. What's most important is what this acrostic psalm does: it lifts up the wonders and perfections of God's Word. The psalm points us to the benefits we receive as we rely on the truths of Scripture.

Icebreaker: What item from your childhood still works today?

Optional follow-up: What features of that item have allowed it to remain reliable over the years?

Optional activity: Provide arts and crafts materials (paper, colored pencils, clay, pipe cleaners, and so on) and encourage participants to create a visual representation of their answer to the icebreaker question.

Video Summary: Robert starts his video message this week with this statement: "It's one thing to believe in the Bible intellectually to be the Word of God. It's another thing to build your life around the truth of Scripture." Psalm 119 addresses the Word of God, its characteristics, and why it is a reliable foundation on which to build our lives. It is an expression of the trustworthiness of all of God's Word. "The word of God is living and effective" (Hebrews 4:12). And it can change our lives.

WATCH THE DVD SEGMENT FOR SESSION 4, THEN USE THE FOLLOWING QUESTIONS AND DISCUSSION POINTS TO TRANSITION INTO THE STUDY.

- Robert offers five ways we can make God's Word a part of our everyday lives: listen, read, study, memorize, and meditate. Which of these areas resonated with you most as something you need to work on?

- Considering these five areas and specifically the one you feel you need to work on most, what are some practical steps you can take to make God's Word a more active part of your life?

WHAT DOES THE BIBLE SAY?

ASK FOR A VOLUNTEER TO READ PSALM 119:1-8,137-144.
Response: What's your initial reaction to these verses?

- What do you like about the text?

- What new application do you hope to receive about building your life on God's Word?

TURN THE GROUP'S ATTENTION TO PSALM 119:137-144.
QUESTION 1: What are some reasons people question the reliability of the Bible?

Answers will vary and may range from more technical reasons regarding proof to more emotional responses related to trust.

Optional follow-up: During what seasons of life have you questioned the reliability of the Bible?
QUESTION 2: What do these verses teach us about God and His Word?

An observation question typically drives the group discussion to the biblical text for greater understanding.

Optional activity: Direct group members to the activity labeled "Reliable Direction" on p. 40. Ask for volunteers to share their responses to how the Bible has proven reliable to them for the topics presented.

MOVE TO PSALM 119:1-8

QUESTION 3: When have you seen the Bible's instruction work?

This question provides an environment and opportunity for the group to share stories and testimony about the powerful truth found in God's Word. Be mindful of group members who may not have accepted Jesus as Savior.

> *Optional follow-up:* What obstacles often hinder people from heeding the Bible's instructions? Why?

QUESTION 4: Why do we follow God's Word?

Challenge the group to go beyond "because it's true." You might ask the group about the difference between *following* God's Word and *believing* God's Word.

> *Optional follow-up:* Why do *you* follow God's Word?

Note: The following question does not appear in the group member book. Use it in your group discussion as time allows.

QUESTION 5: What steps will you take in the near future to increasingly build your life on God's Word?

This is an application question included to move members toward definitive action.

> *Optional follow-up:* What steps can we take as a group to support each other in this goal?

LIVE IT OUT

When the writer called the Lord "righteous," he ascribed to Him a consistency of character in which there is no deviation. Direct group member to how they can build their lives on this altogether right God.

- **Schedule time to read God's Word.** To discover how God blesses, start with Proverbs and read a chapter each day for a month. Do at least one of the proverbs that very day.

- **Dig deeper.** Read chapter 2, "How Can I Know the Bible is True?" in *How Can I Know?* by Robert Jeffress. Invite others to read and discuss it with you.

- **Disciple a new believer.** Coach someone else in developing a lifelong habit of Bible reading and study.

Challenge: Commit to identifying three blessings from God before lunch, three before supper, and three before bed. This builds an eye for recognizing God at work. Consider writing them down so you can revisit them later.

Pray: Ask for prayer requests and ask group members to pray for the different requests as intercessors. As the leader, close this time by asking the Lord to help each of you personalize and apply His Word to your lives.

SESSION FIVE: HOW DID WE GET HERE AND WHY?

The Point: The universe is here because God spoke.

The Passage: Genesis 1:1-3,6,9,11,14,20,26-27

The Setting: Genesis is the book of beginnings, and this account starts with the beginning of creation. God created the universe by His own creative power and He deemed good every aspect of what He created.

Icebreaker: In all creation, what is most intriguing to you?

Optional activity: If your meeting place allows it, lead the group outside and encourage them to observe different aspects of the natural world. Ask the following questions while still outside:

- What do you find intriguing right here? Why?

- What emotions do you typically experience when you immerse yourself in creation?

- What are some elements of creation about which you'd like to learn more?

Video Summary: "God created man in His own image; He created him in the image of God" (Genesis 1:27). Robert opens and closes this week's message with a reminder that we are not here by accident. We were created by God, in His image, for a purpose. Generally speaking, as believers, we are here to glorify God. More specifically, we are here to fulfill God's agenda—He wants to save people from sin and He calls us to be a part of that.

WATCH THE DVD SEGMENT FOR SESSION 5, THEN USE THE FOLLOWING QUESTIONS AND DISCUSSION POINTS TO TRANSITION INTO THE STUDY.

- God created the universe, and He created us uniquely for His purposes. What desires has God placed in your heart? What is it you are passionate about?

- What are the unique gifts God has given you?

- In what ways do you see these things working together in your life?

WHAT DOES THE BIBLE SAY?

ASK FOR A VOLUNTEER TO READ ALOUD GENESIS 1:1-3,6,9,11,14,20,26-27.
Response: What's your initial reaction to these verses?

- What questions do you have about these verses?

- What new application do you hope to get from this passage?

TURN THE GROUP'S ATTENTION TO GENESIS 1:1-3,6,9,11,14,20.
QUESTION 1: Why does it matter what we believe about the origins of the universe?

Not only are people usually willing to enter into these kinds of cosmic debates, but our understanding of the universe impacts our understanding of practically everything else.

Optional follow-up: Which of the six journalistic questions—who, what, when, where, why, and how—are addressed in Genesis 1?

QUESTION 2: What can we learn about our Creator from the opening verses of the Bible?

This question asks group members to look more closely at a passage that they have probably read many times before. Encourage the group to look in the details for clues about Who God is.

Optional follow-up: What can we learn about ourselves from these same verses?

MOVE TO GENESIS 1:26-27.

QUESTION 3: What feelings are stirred up when you read that you are made in the image of God?

Be prepared to give your own answer. The intent is to get the group talking about themselves as God's unique image bearers and what it means to bear the image of the Creator of the universe.

> *Optional follow-up:* What does it mean to be created in God's image?

QUESTION 4: How does the fact that we are God's image bearers influence what we say and do?

The group is being asked to apply life to biblical truth with their answers, specifically how we can live out being created in God's image.

> *Optional activity:* Direct group members to the activity labeled "Created with Purpose" on p. 51. Ask volunteers to share their responses to how what they do matters—at home, at church, and in their community.

Note: The following question does not appear in the group member book. Use it in your group discussion as time allows.

QUESTION 5: How does knowing you were created in God's image affect your relationship with God and your relationship with others?

The group has already spent time talking about what it means and how it feels to be God's image bearers. This question will give them an opportunity to process how this truth affects how they relate to God and to others.

LIVE IT OUT

The Bible points us to an all-powerful and personal Creator. Direct group members to three ways this reality can influence their lives.

- **Trust God with your circumstances.** Since God can speak a universe into existence, He can be trusted with your life.
- **See people as God sees them.** Just as you are created in God's image, so is everyone else. Lead someone to discover the value God has placed on him or her.
- **Value God's creation.** We don't worship nature, but identify ways you can care for God's creation.

Challenge: Read the Book of John. Journal what you learn about the image of God and how to reflect it in your own life.

Pray: Ask for prayer requests and ask group members to pray for the different requests as intercessors. As the leader, close this time by asking the Lord to help each of you live your lives in a way that communicates your belief in the truth that you were created in the image of the God of the universe.

SESSION SIX: IF GOD IS GOOD, WHY IS THERE SUFFERING?

The Point: God meets us in our suffering.

The Passage: Job 30:26-31; 42:1-6

The Setting: God allowed Satan to test Job through intense suffering. Satan took away Job's children and possessions and later attacked his health. Job's friends presented the view that we suffer because we sin, but

Job maintained his uprightness. When God spoke, He never addressed Job's suffering but spoke only of His sovereignty. Job repented of questioning God's goodness, and he experienced the gracious deliverance of God.

Icebreaker: What makes life better when you feel lousy?

>*Optional follow-up:* When has someone gone the extra mile to cheer you up?

>*Optional activity:* Prepare a selection of "comfort foods" before the group meeting—apple pie, chicken soup, chocolate-chip cookies, mashed potatoes, and so on. Encourage group members to describe their emotional reaction to each food they sample.

Video Summary: In his video message this week, Robert points out that often our question about why God allows suffering really means, *Why do You allow suffering in **my** world?* No one is exempt. We see proof of this all the way through the Bible—Joseph, Paul, Peter, and Jesus. "You will have suffering in this world. Be courageous! I have conquered the world" (John 16:33). The Book of Job, our focal passage for this week's study, never answers why there is suffering. But it does assure us that God is sovereign, He is in control, and nothing happens without a purpose. God allows affliction and hardship so that we can experience the grace and love of God.

WATCH THE DVD SEGMENT FOR SESSION 6, THEN USE THE FOLLOWING QUESTIONS AND DISCUSSION POINTS TO TRANSITION INTO THE STUDY.

- The Book of Job reminds us that there are some unanswerable questions in life, especially related to suffering. How do you handle your unanswerable questions?

- As believers we know the end of the story—that God will one day defeat suffering. In what ways does this truth impact the way you deal with suffering?

WHAT DOES THE BIBLE SAY?

ASK FOR A VOLUNTEER TO READ ALOUD JOB 30:26-31; 42:1-6.
Response: What's your initial reaction to these verses?

- What questions do you have about suffering?

- What new application do you hope to get from this passage?

TURN THE GROUP'S ATTENTION TO JOB 30:26-31.
QUESTION 1: What is it we question about God when we read these verses?

Answers may include God's indifference, why He allows bad things to happen to good people, and the presence of suffering in the world.

>*Optional activity:* Direct group members to the activity labeled "What Do I Do?" on p. 59. Ask for volunteers to share their response to one of the three options.

MOVE TO JOB 42:1-3.
QUESTION 2: What has caused you to question God's wisdom or power?

Answers will range from a personal story or testimony to an event from someone else's life, perhaps a relative or close friend of a group member. Doubts are not uncommon even in the life of a believer.

Optional follow-up: Read Job 40:1-14 to see some of what Job was responding to. What's your reaction to God's words and approach in this passage?

QUESTION 3: How have you been changed by an encounter with God?

This is an opportunity for the group to look at Job's unique experience and apply it to their own lives. This is also an opportunity for group members to share about a time when God might have shown them that they didn't know as much as they thought they did.

Optional follow-up: What does it mean to "repent"?

Optional follow-up: When have you experienced a desire to repent? What happened next?

CONTINUE WITH JOB 42:4-6.

QUESTION 4: What can we do to express faith in the midst of suffering?

Be sure the group looks to Job as the model for expressing faith in the midst of suffering. Think specifically of ways suffering can move us closer to God. Responses to this application question will vary.

Optional follow-up: What steps can we take to search for God in the midst of our suffering?

Note: The following question does not appear in the group member book. Use it in your group discussion as time allows.

QUESTION 5: Given everything we've discussed, how can we reconcile God's goodness with the reality of suffering?

You've discussed God's goodness, dealing with doubts, how Job handled his trials, and the nature of suffering. The goal of this question is to get the group to acknowledge the reality that we live in a fallen world but we don't have to face this reality alone.

LIVE IT OUT

Determine to meet suffering armed with God's love and presence, "casting all your cares on Him, because He cares about you" (1 Pet. 5:7). Guide group members to look at three of the many ways to do this.

- **Refuse despair.** It's OK to grieve, but that doesn't mean we have to despair. Trust God's love and goodness.

- **Be there.** You often don't have to say a word, but your presence can be a great comfort to those suffering.

- **Help.** Connect with a friend or two to minister to families suffering through illness, hospitalization, or the death of a loved one. Develop a list of needs, and enlist other volunteers to help meet these needs as long as necessary.

Challenge: God meets us in our suffering. We can also meet one another in suffering. Think of ways you can deliver God's care to people who are suffering this week. Then keep your eyes open for those who may need your help.

Pray: As the leader, close this final session of *Honest to God* in prayer. Ask the Lord to help each of you as you move forward to use the principles you have learned in this study to live out what the Bible says about crucial issues.

WHERE THE BIBLE MEETS LIFE

Bible Studies for Life™ will help you know Christ, live in community, and impact the world around you. If you enjoyed this study, be sure and check out these forthcoming releases.* Six sessions each.

TITLE	RELEASE DATE
Do Over: Experience New Life in Christ *by Ben Mandrell*	September 2013
Honest to God: Real Questions People Ask *by Robert Jeffress*	September 2013
Let Hope In *by Pete Wilson*	December 2013
Productive: Finding Joy in Work *by Ronnie and Nick Floyd*	December 2013
Resilient Faith: Standing Strong in the Midst of Suffering *by Mary Jo Sharp*	March 2014
Beyond Belief *by Freddy Cardoza*	March 2014
Overcome: Living Beyond Your Circumstances *by Alex Himaya*	June 2014
Connected: My Life in the Church *by Thom S. Rainer*	June 2014

If your group meets regularly, you might consider Bible Studies for Life as an ongoing series. Available for your entire church—kids, students, and adults—it's a format that will be a more affordable option over time. And you can jump in anytime. For more information, visit **biblestudiesforlife.com**.

biblestudiesforlife.com/smallgroups
800.458.2772 | LifeWay Christian Stores

Title and release dates subject to change.
*This is not a complete list of releases. Additional titles will continue to be released every three months. Visit website for more information.